# 123 Steps Of Life Goals Achievement

## WITH CASE STUDIES

OLUFEMI AYINDE

## ABOUT THIS BOOK

I have put in steps the Lord mentioned in the Bible, documented experience of some multi-millionaires and personal life experience, so that this book will open your eyes, change your thinking, your mentality and enable you to move forward in life.

I want people that read this book to know that both success and goals setting are difficult to set and achieved for many reasons. Many people come to this world without achieving their goals in life, while few were able to achieve their goals. I believe we need to borrow the ideas of those who achieved their goals and follow the foot prints to achieve our own. ***"To what gain is a man who came to this world without achieving his purpose in life?" his next generation will not forgive him.***

Start right now to set and achieve your goals while reading this book with life case studies as your back up experience.

## ON THE MARBLE

"Champions focus on where they are going while losers focus on what they passing through in life".

## ON THE MARBLE

"When you replay the past, you will poison the present".

| CONTENTS | Page |
|---|---|
| Definition Of Goals | 5 |
| What Are The Needed Steps? | 6 |
| Write Your Goal Down | 7 |
| Be Focused | 8 |
| Renew Your Mind | 9 |
| Be A Champion | 14 |
| Never Give Up | 15 |
| Invest In Yourself | 19 |
| Maintain Your Integrity | 20 |
| Make Positive Confessions | 24 |
| Avoid Negative People | 25 |
| Never Postpone A Thing | 26 |
| Dare To Believe In What God Can Do Through You. | 27 |
| Have A Plan | 28 |
| Stand Alone, If You Have To | 29 |
| Pick A Mentor | 30 |
| Trust No Man | 31 |
| Take Reasonable Risks | 32 |
| Read Good Books | 33 |
| Keep Trying | 35 |

*"Once we make a decision, all things will come to us"*

## DEFINITION OF GOALS

A goal is a desired target, an objective, something that you hope to achieve.

To design the life you want. Your goal in life may look so difficult but I want to tell you that no matter how difficult your goal may look, it can be achieved if only you know the principles and you have faith. Make sure you do not set unrealistic goals.

A goal is a dream in action with a purpose.

## WHAT ARE THE NEEDED STEPS?

The following steps are necessary to achieve your set goals and to change the course of your life.

### BEGIN WITH PRAYER

1. Soak your goals with prayer.

2. You must pray always for God's protection and guidance. (Ps 119:18)

3. You must water your goals with prayer: after setting your goals in life you must water them with prayer every day. Goals are like plants, they need daily attention and constant care so that they will not die

4. You must re-evaluate your goal periodically: you need checkpoints on the way to reaching your goals, check your progress to see how you are doing.

# HAVE A VISION

5. You must discern the dimensions of success: God himself is a goal setter. Have a vision of what type of success you want. Then desire such.

6. You must know where you are going and what to do at the right time.

7. Develop a mental picture of your goal. You must have a picture of what you want and envision it with your spiritual eyes every day.

## WRITE YOUR GOAL DOWN

8. You must write down your goals: Hab 2:2 says write down your dreams and your goals. Make it plain on paper so that others can understand you.

9. Plan to be a champion and a winner in life and not a loser.

## BE FOCUSED

10. Focus is when your interest or your attention is directed at something. What you must do is to be focused on. When you are focused, you will not be wandering all about without achievement.

11. Do not jump from one business to the other because somebody is making it. But ask God what he wants you to do in life and the type of business to do not imitate anybody: because all imitations are fake not original. Just be yourself.

## KNOW YOUR DIRECTION

12. You must know that a life without direction is a life without aim. The most difficult man to discourage is a man that knows where he is going. You can never discourage him because he knows where he is going.

13. Make goals balanced and reasonable: many people fear the setting of goals because they think they might not make it. Remember always that impossible is a word in the dictionary of fools and you are not a fool.

## RENEW YOUR MIND

14.     Remember that nobody is a failure until he or she begins to fail from within. Tell yourself that you can do it.

15.     Do not be afraid of anything no matter the situation you find yourself, stay focused on your set goal.

16.     Remember that no condition is permanent in life.

**ON THE MARBLE**

"A successful life often involves seasons of pain"

**ON THE MARBLE**

"The quality of your wisdom will determine the quality of your decisions"

17. Do not accept defeat in life or in your set goal.

18. You must eliminate any negative thinking in your life.

19. See any failure in your life as feedback: Also see problems as opportunities.

20. You must have positive attitudes. Do not develop attitudes that will make people to be running away from you.

21. Continue to think of victory and not defeat. When you always think of victory, all the resources of nature will flow towards enabling you to achieve victory and success in life. Remember, the bible says as a man thinketh in his heart, so he is.

22. Always see God bigger than your problem and troubles in life.

23. Believe that you are unstoppable, that even the devil can not stop your goal in life.

24. Always maintain a position attitude.

25. You must not forget that any goal setter is an achiever, just believe that you will make it in life.

26. Your goal may be difficult but still believe and move forward. The Bible says, the latter end of it shall be big. (Job 8:7)

27. Remember that adversities are stepping stones to success – you may not understand this saying but it is real, because I am talking and writing for my personal experience in life.

## BE A CHAMPION

28.     Remember that champions focus on where they are going and how to make it, while losers focus on what they are passing through in life.

## MEDITATE ON THE SCRIPTURE

29.     The mentality of God is always through simply reading the scripture. Just read and meditate on the word of God always: Joshua 1:8

## SEE OBSTACLES AS NORMAL

30. Most times before you achieve success: there must be obstacles to hinder you from achieving your set goals in life. I also want you to know that there is no way you can get to the Promised Land without passing through the wilderness.

31. Adversities are stepping stones to success: your worst circumstance may be God's best opportunity to bless you.

32. Human beings can stop you temporally but I want you to know that you are the only one that can stop yourself permanently. The Bible says for as a man thinkest in his heart so he is.

## NEVER GIVE UP

33. Go for anything you want in your life: in as much as it is in line with God, just plan for your life and never give up until you get it.

## FEAR NOT

**"Do the thing you are afraid to do and the death of fear is certain"**

## TRUST GOD

**"I need to take an emotional breath, step back and remind myself who actually in-charge of my life is**

34. Discover your mentors, especially spiritual mentors, who are spirit filled: do not choose a voice as your mentor because the Bible says a blind man cannot lead blind man.

35. Pursue and follow quality people in life

36. Spend time with great men and women who have made it in life and listen to their stories in life and their experiences. Proverb 13:20 says, he that moves with wise men shall be wise.

37. Make no plan to go backward in your goal setting: The book of Isaiah says woe to them that go back to Egypt. (Isaiah 31:1)

38. Position yourself in a place where people will favor you. Do not hide. A golden fish has no hiding place.

## INVEST IN YOURSELF

39. Invest in yourself: spend time, effort, and money developing your mind, spirit and inner man.

40. Find out what you are good at: Take a good look at yourself. Find out what it is and begin to do exploit in it.

41. Most people are accountable to God for developing your skill (Matt 25:14-35) Study people with similar talents and what makes them successful. Learn from them.

42. Attend seminars and programs. Ask questions from people that are higher than you. Nobody knows everything.

43. Do not follow gossips and talebearers, nor make them your friends: The Bible says blessed is he that walketh not in the counsel of the ungodly nor sitteth in the seat of the scornful (Psalm 1:1-3).

44. Admire men and women that achieve their goals in life. You can do so by reading their books and listening to their messages.

## MAINTAIN YOUR INTEGRITY

45. Be honest and sincere in anything you are doing: The Bible says let your yes be yes and let your no be no.

46. Always insist on integrity: it is only what you say you will do. Demand it and let others see it in you.

47.  Accept corrections: You too can make mistakes. Do not be a know all.

48.  Do not give wrong counsel or advice to someone: The Bible says that whatever a man sows, he will reap (Gal. 6:6-7) So if you give wrong counsel to some one, by and by it must come back to you. E.g. Ahitophel and Absalom.

49.  Be punctual in anything you are involved and be committed. Do not form the habit of going l

## ON THE MARBLE

"Better a poor man who walks in his integrity, than a rich man who is perverse in his ways"

-

Proverbs 28:6

# TAKE RISKS

"For everything you have, you have gained

Something else; and for everything you gain, you

Loose something else".

## MAKE POSITIVE CONFESSIONS

50. You must bridle your tongue: The Bible says that death and life are in the tongue. (Proverb 18: 21)

51. Never you confessed negative in life and any condition you find yourself do not permit any word of discouragement in your mouth.

## AVOID NEGATIVE PEOPLE

63. Never discuss your goals with someone who has no goal in life, he will discourage you or even stop you. The Bible says that as a man thinks in his heart, so he is.

64. Do not be confused by negative people or negative or negative situation in life.

65. Remember that your belief will determine what you will get or achieve.

66. Always reflect on the victories of Bible champions: e.g. David, who killed Goliath with a single shot by faith, and eventually became king (Psalm 17). Joseph overcame the hatred of his brothers and false accusations and became second in power to Pharaoh. (Gen 37:41). So you can equally overcome any problem in your life and achieve your goal like a champion.

67. Remember that your worst circumstance may be God's best opportunity to bless and lift you up.

68. Re-program your mind once in a while and see if there is any where you want.

69. Make God your partner in life, always depend on God and put your confidence in him.

## NEVER POSTPONE A THING

70. Avoid procrastination in anything. Procrastination is major enemy of progress in life.

## DARE TO BELIEVE IN WHAT GOD CAN DO THROUGH YOU.

71. Do not blame yourself for any failure in life but learn from your mistakes and move forward.

72. Never give up in life. Believe that with God all things are possible. Your failure is not your final.

73. Learn how to carve ordinary into the extra ordinary.

74. Always believe that your future begins right now with your goal.

75. Always believe that your goals should be specific, solid and serious. Bear in mind that goals should have dead lines.

76. Goals should be out of reach but within sight. If your goals are number one priority, then you will find time and effort to make it happen.

77. Aim high low aim lead to low achievement.

## HAVE A PLAN

78. Remember that you can not accomplished more than.

80. You must be creative: flood your life with ideas form many sources.

## STAND ALONE, IF YOU HAVE TO

81. You must have willingness to stand alone: where other people are running away from the problem of life, stand alone.

82. You must discover your own particular talent.

83. You must be honest and always stand on the truth.

84. Do not worry much about any problem in life, because problems are inevitable.

85. Do not be Mr. know all: you must admit mistakes and be ready to correct yourself.

86. Do not involve yourself in any corrupt practice of or immoral act that will dent your image or even destroy your integrity.

## PICK A MENTOR

87. You must have spiritual guidance and coverage.

## BE A CHEERFUL GIVER

88. You must be generous: be a giver and not a stingy person. The arms you are giving to people can make a way for you. Act 9:36-40 tells us of a giving woman called Dorcas. She was not stingy.

89. You must have compassion on the needy especially orphans and other less privileged people.

## TRUST NO MAN

90. Do not trust any man so mush: Even God says that he regretted making man. (Gen 6:5-6)

91. Do not have a tight relationship with any man: because the person you call your friend or your best friend today can be your worst enemy tomorrow. The Bible says that the heart of man is deceitful and desperately wicked who can know except God.

92. Do not be a complainant. If you complain too much you will loose your strength and confidence in God. The Bible says that if you faint on the day of adversity, your strength is small.

93. Do not look at the size of any problem in your life: but believe that you can

overcome any problem you face. The Bible says that he that observes the wind shall not sow

## TAKE REASONABLE RISKS

1. Remember that you must take risks in life before you make it. The life you are living is a risk; anything can happen at any time.

2. Do not believe that your background will stop you: there was a man in the Bible by name Jephta. He was son of a harlot but he did not allow his background to stop him. (Judge 1:1-15)

# READ GOOD BOOKS

3. Do not read the book and his of failures: but read the book of champions and warriors who made it in life.

4. Celebrate yourself anytime in any situation – believe that you are the best man or woman on earth. If you are a short man, celebrate yourself, if you are tall, you are the best man or woman on earth: the most important thing is to begin setting goal

5. Be strong and courageous. Also work hard: life only celebrates achievers not observers and losers, People will only remember you for what you achieve not what you observed or what you lost.

6. Be genuine in anything you are doing in life.

7. Always believe that your case is different.

8. Your must forget the past failure and move forward: do not be stuck on any ship. The Lord told Moses in the Bible that he should

tell the children of Israel to move forward. (Ex 14:13)

9. Stop looking back: you must stop remembering how you fell. Anyone that is moving forward and keeps looking back will surely fall into a ditch: so let your eyes be focused on the future: the Bible says remember not the past things. (Isaiah 43:18)

## KEEP TRYING

10. Do not give up, even when you encounter failure in your life, keep trying until you succeed. The Bible says that a righteous man falleth seven times and riseth seven times- Proverbs

## FORGIVE OTHERS

11. You must have a forgiving heart: when you forgive those that offend you, then God will forgive your sin and have mercy upon you. (Mark 11: 25- 26)

> With God and he will not allow you to fail in life.

12. Withdraw yourself from contentious people: a contentious person is a trouble maker and you can never achieve your goal in life by making trouble.

**FORGET THE PAST**

13. When you replay the past, you will poison the present.

14. Forgetting the past is the weapon that wins battle of the past: it is the weapon that has kept marriages together; it is the weapon that wins any battles and achieves goals.

15. It is your personal responsibility to motivate yourself toward your dream and goals in your life.

# MISCELLANEOUS

16. Make sure you put faith signs in your home, your office and your shop: what you see determines what you feel and what you will achieve.

17. Focus your mind on the rewards of finishing a task- faith because their focus is on the finished result and their achievement in life.

18. Remember that failure does not always occur because of what you do, but because of something that you failed to do.

19. You must know that a successful life is often expensive: it must cost you something to become a champion and to achieve your goal.

20. Successful life often involve seasons of pains. Your new revelation or new ideas may expose errors in your childhood teaching.

21. Do not change what you believe until your belief system cannot produce something you want.

22. You must make out time to pursue your dreams and goals.

23. Impossible things happen to those who expect them to happen.

24. You must be a man of great expectation: believing that anything is possible before God.

25. Remember that there is no new thing on earth: history repeats itself: so whatever that happens to you must have happened to someone before you. (Ecc 1:9)

26. Champions are crowned after they defeat an enemy: so to be a champion you must achieve your goal.

27. Do not boast to everybody about your ability to overcome. When you overcome, the people will see it for themselves.

28. Attends life changing seminars and follow up with what you learn.

29. Be courageous to express yourself with your business proposal with anybody that you think could be your client, never be discourage when you meet some road blocks.

## IN CONCLUSION

God bless you the more. I will see you at the top as you begin today to set goals for yourself, ministering and loved ones. A life without goals is a life without purpose.

# CASE STUDY 1

Mr. John was a graduate looking for job, he has written many application letters but he could not get a job. His condition was so bad that he decided to go to a garage park and beg a commercial bus driver to work with him as a bus conductor.

Luckily one accept him and he started conducting for him and on the second day, he was beaten up by a passage right inside the bus on change issue and he could not see properly for some days. The owner of the bus got aware of the matter; Mr. John was sacked and sent back to the labor market.

Some months later, he picked up a job in a commercial bank as a clerical officer. Every single day, he will read some motivational book and Bible. He picks up an idea of setting up an assets management company and he registered his company and he decided to resign from the bank.

The last salary that he received from the bank was sowed to God as dedicated offering and he has nothing on him. He told his wife and his little children about his decision to start up his own business but they were not happy knowing that the hardship will be too much on them, but they have no choice than to accept.

He called on two friends to join him in the business, at times when they have no transport fees they will treck to client office and when they return, he will share his food with them. They have reduce their outing to two days in a week because of transport fee and what he received as commission will be share into three parts. He has to withdraw his children from big school to small school because of the school fees and he told them not send them home for school fees that anytime has money he will pay.

They suffer for four years before they could get a client with one million investment fund and gradually things start to change for them. From their commission, they were able to buy a fairly used car that produce thick smoke once the engine is on. God have mercy on them when he came across an old friend, who gave him 1.5 million to buy a new car but instead of him to buy a new car, he sold off the fairly use car that he was using and added some money to buy another fairly use car that is better than the one he was using and invest the rest of the money on stock. Luckily, the stock price jump time 4 and later time 10. The story has change and he never for once missed to pay tithes and offering in the church. He went to a church to worship on one Sunday and the pastor of the church begin to look for him and trace him to his own church and said, Mr. so you too is a pastor, ever since we started our church we never received such a big amount from a donor as tithes and that is why I come to say thank you and he smile back at him.

His assets management company has covered the whole country with over 2,000 staffs and he has bought cars and built houses for over 100 staffs with the corporate at the commercial nerves of the country. He is currently managing the federal government assets and he is a multi-millionaire.

# CASE 2

Mr. Robert is another example who retired early at age of 47years old. He got married to his beautiful wife Mrs. Kim Robert, they both started as authors of motivational books in united state. He owed a total debt of $400,000 and they were both living in basement giving to him by one of his friends.

The story did not change immediately but not until their 7th book, The Rich dad Poor dad. Which sold millions of copies in 57 countries and he was 2 time Amazon hall of fame award and 6 years best seller award on the wall street and he has sold more than 17 million copies altogether. He is a founder of cash-flow Company.

OLUFEMI AYINDE

Olufemi_ayinde@yahoo.com

OR

Topeayinde05@gmail.com

# **Other Books**

www.ingramcontent.com/pod-product-compliance
Lightning Source LLC
Chambersburg PA
CBHW080608190526
45169CB00007B/2929